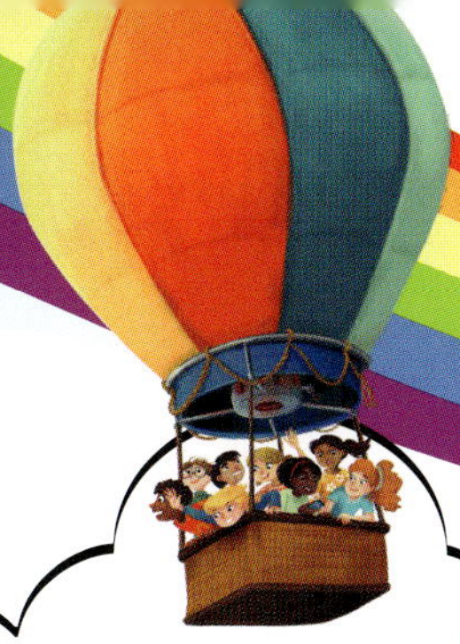

Dropping In On...
Denver

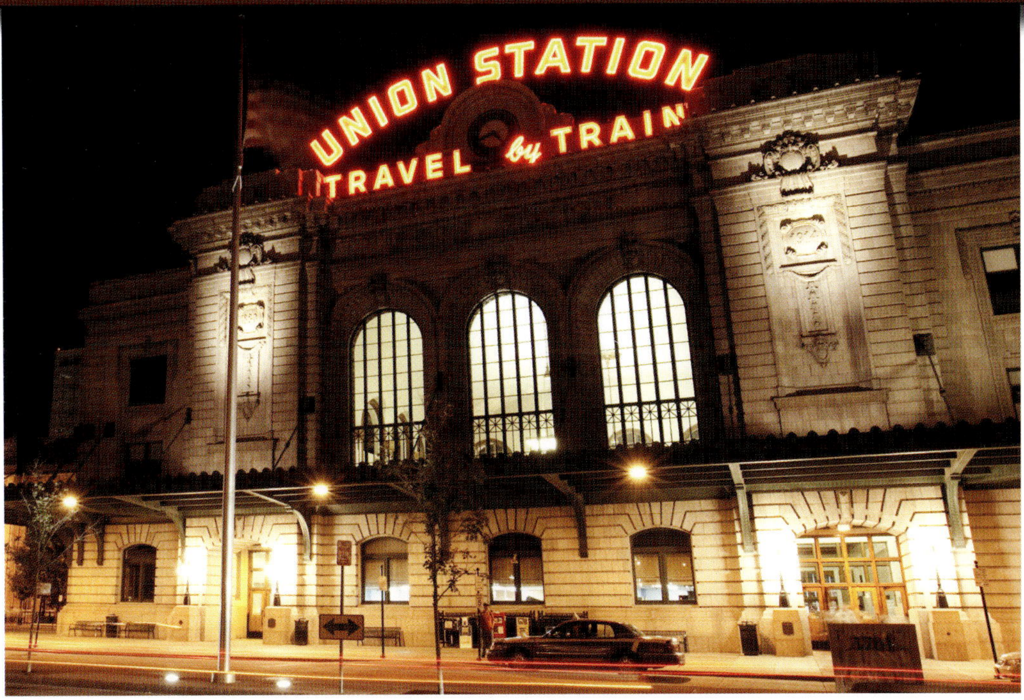

Hilarie Staton

Educational Media

rourkeeducationalmedia.com

Scan for Related Titles and Teacher Resources

Before & After Reading Activities

Before Reading:

Building Academic Vocabulary and Background Knowledge

Before reading a book, it is important to tap into what your child or students already know about the topic. This will help them develop their vocabulary, increase their reading comprehension, and make connections across the curriculum.

1. Look at the cover of the book. What will this book be about?
2. What do you already know about the topic?
3. Let's study the Table of Contents. What will you learn about in the book's chapters?
4. What would you like to learn about this topic? Do you think you might learn about it from this book? Why or why not?
5. Use a reading journal to write about your knowledge of this topic. Record what you already know about the topic and what you hope to learn about the topic.
6. Read the book.
7. In your reading journal, record what you learned about the topic and your response to the book.
8. After reading the book complete the activities below.

Content Area Vocabulary
Read the list. What do these words mean?

conflict
factories
foothills
miners
ore
plains
smelters
suburbs
tourists
transcontinental

After Reading:

Comprehension and Extension Activity

After reading the book, work on the following questions with your child or students in order to check their level of reading comprehension and content mastery.

1. What jobs did people do when Denver was just a small town? (Summarize)
2. Why did so many people travel through Denver on their way to the Rocky Mountains? (Infer)
3. How did businesses help Denver grow? (Asking questions)
4. What outdoor activities would you like to do if you visited Denver? (Text to self connection)
5. Why have people moved to Denver? (Asking questions)

Extension Activity

Create a travel brochure about Denver. Include several places visitors should see. Write short, exciting paragraphs that highlight the most interesting things about the city. And don't forget to add pictures! You can draw them or print them out from the Internet.

Table of Contents

Between the Plains and the Mountains 4

Fighting to Become Number One 11

Rocky Mountain Metropolis 14

More to Do 23

Timeline 29

Glossary 30

Index 31

Show What You Know 31

Websites to Visit 31

About the Author 32

Denver Facts

Founded: 1858
Land area: 153 square miles (246.23 square kilometers)
Elevation: 5,280 feet or 1 mile (1,609 meters)
Population: 682,545 (2015)
Average Daytime Temperatures:
winter: 47 degrees Fahrenheit (8 degrees Celsius)
spring: 63 degrees Fahrenheit (17 degrees Celsius)
summer: 83 degrees Fahrenheit (28 degrees Celsius)
fall: 66 degrees Fahrenheit (19 degrees Celsius)

Ethnic Diversity:
African-American 13.3%
American Indian or Alaska Native 1.2%
Asian 5.6%
Native Hawaiian or Pacific Islander 0.2%
Hispanic or Latino 17.6%
White 63.7%

City Nicknames:
Queen City of the Plains
The Queen of the Plains
Queen City of the West
Mile High City
Convention City
Wall Street of the West

Number of Annual Visitors: 15.4 million

Between the Plains and the Mountains

Denver, Colorado, was built along streams and rivers on the high, flat, grassy **plains**. Nearby are the **foothills** of the Rocky Mountains. The Front Range Mountains, part of the Rocky Mountains, are the closest to Denver. They are some of the highest mountains on the eastern side of the Rockies.

MOST PEOPLE THINK DENVER IS IN THE MOUNTAINS. IT ISN'T! IT IS ON FLAT LAND, CALLED PLAINS, IN THE MIDDLE OF THE UNITED STATES.

Millions of years ago, dinosaurs wandered this area. After they disappeared, mammoths, giant bison, and even camels lived here.

At Dinosaur Ridge you can see dinosaur footprints dried in the mud and bones still in the ground.

The Rocky Mountains affect life on the plains. They are so tall and the mountainsides so steep, they make travel difficult. They also affect the weather. Most days in Denver are sunny with little rain or snow. They have mild winters with a warm wind that melts any snow they get.

Denver Notes
In 1982 Denver got almost 24 inches (61 centimeters) of snow in 24 hours. The wind blew the snow until it was over 120 inches (304.5 centimeters) high in some places!

At first, American Indians lived in the area, but not all year. The Comanche camped there until they began using horses. Then they spent more time further out on the Great Plains. The Arapahoe and Cheyenne camped and hunted near where Denver is today.

At Denver's Museum of Nature & Science you can learn about the American Indians who lived in the area.

In 1803, much of Colorado became part of the United States. It was included in the Kansas Territory. Later it was made into the separate Colorado Territory. Small towns grew around the South Platte River.

A few trading posts were built for the American Indians and fur traders who trapped beaver in the Rockies.

Denver is on the high plains, 5,332 feet (1,625 meters) above sea level. That's one mile (1.6 kilometers) up, so it's called The Mile High City.

Denver Notes

General Larimer named his town Denver to honor the governor of the Kansas Territory. When the news arrived in Kansas, Denver was no longer governor, but the town kept the name.

Then, in 1858, William Green Russell found some gold in nearby Cherry Creek. Immediately many **miners** came. Most soon left because so little gold was found. Others stayed, so the small town grew.

Denver was a long way from anywhere. Its people wanted their town to be the most important one around. When Denver became a stagecoach stop, businesses opened so travelers, farmers, and miners could shop. Denver joined with other small towns and kept growing.

Try your hand at gold panning when you visit the historic stagecoach stop, house, and farm in Denver's Four Mile Park.

In 1864, after several years of **conflict**, the Arapahoe and Cheyenne were peacefully camped at Sand Creek, south of Denver. A troop of the United States military attacked these American Indians without reason. More than 150 people were killed. Most were women and children.

Fighting to Become Number One

The region's farms and mines continued to grow. Denver's businesses sold supplies to nearby miners, farmers and ranchers. They sold farm animals, seeds, and equipment. Mills ground the farmer's wheat into flour. Denver businessmen built banks to keep and lend money.

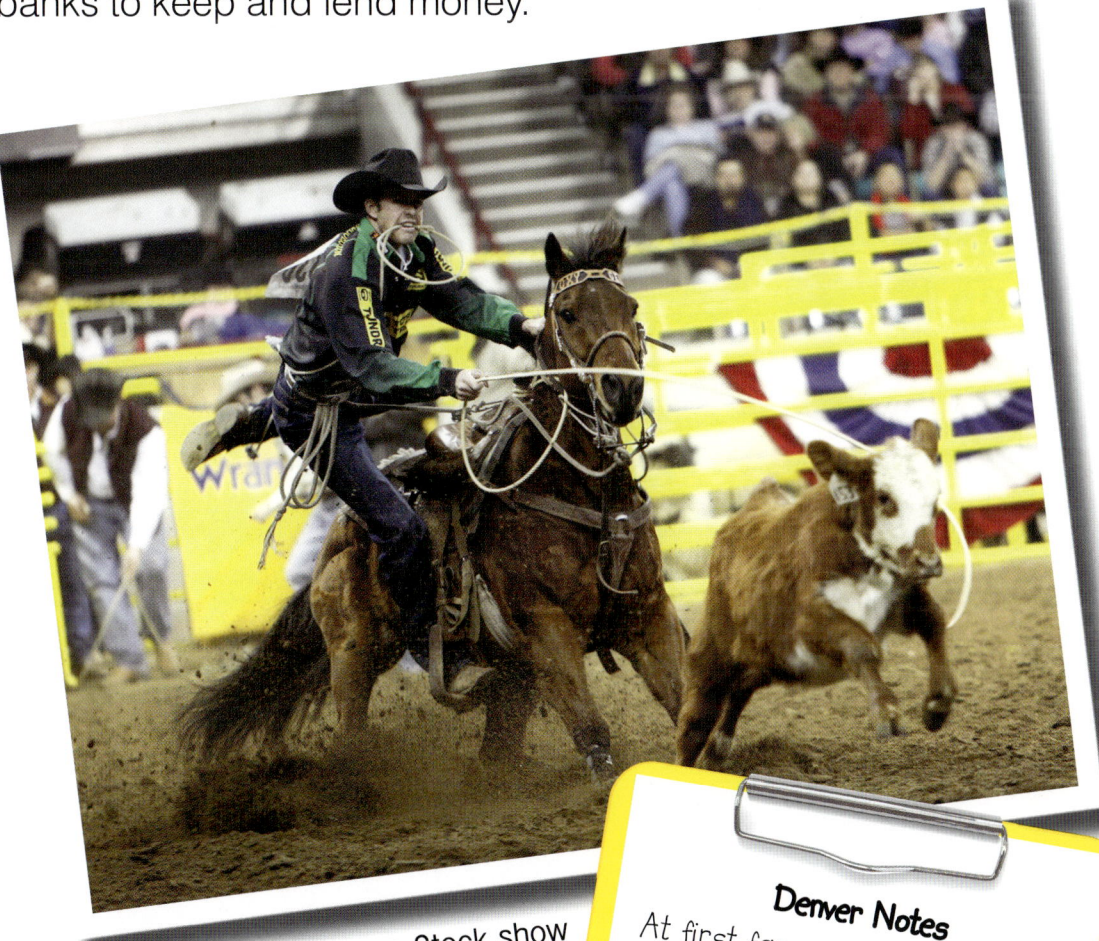

The National Western Stock show was first held in Denver in 1906. Now it includes a rodeo, too.

Denver Notes

At first farmers grew wheat on the plains around Denver. Later, they began growing sugar beets. These were used to make sugar.

In 1866, the **transcontinental** railroad was built in Wyoming. It could not be built near Denver because of the nearby steep mountains. So Denver businessmen built their own railroad. They connected it with the one in Wyoming. Soon, other railroads were built to Denver. Denver became the "Queen of the Plains."

Denver was finally connected to the towns on the eastern side of the Rocky Mountains. Miners sold their gold and silver **ore** in Denver. They bought their supplies there. **Factories** began to make machines for mines. They also built **smelters** to clean and melt the ore instead of sending it to the east.

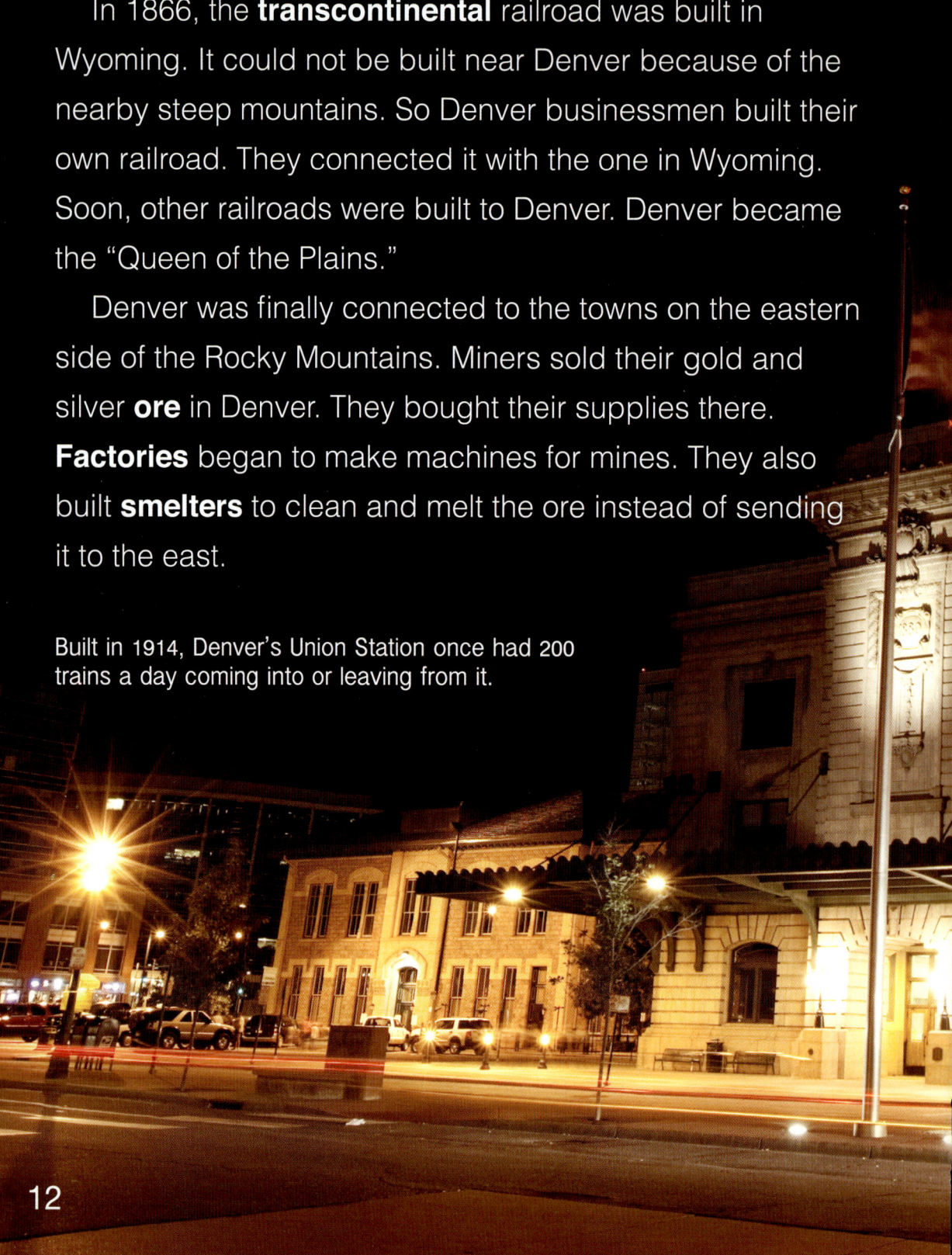

Built in 1914, Denver's Union Station once had 200 trains a day coming into or leaving from it.

The History Colorado Center has a diorama that shows what Denver looked like in 1860.

Rocky Mountain Metropolis

When Colorado became a state, the town of Golden was its capital. But ten years later, the capital moved to Denver. The governor worked in the beautiful new capitol building. The legislature still meets here.

People traveled to Denver for many reasons. Some went to find work. Others went because they were sick and the climate helped them get well. Many remained in the city and helped it grow. Some were just **tourists** who headed to the mountains.

The Colorado capitol building was built with stone and gold from Colorado.

Denver Notes
Colorado became a state in 1876. The United States was celebrating its 100th birthday. That's why Colorado is called The Centennial State!

Home of J.J. and Molly Brown, built in 1889. J. J. Brown discovered gold and became a millionaire. His wife, the "unsinkable" Molly Brown, became a hero saving people as the *Titanic* sank in 1912.

DENVER WAS THE FIRST LARGE CITY IN THE WORLD WHERE WOMEN COULD VOTE!

Denver's businesses and factories needed many workers. Some Chinese workers settled in Denver after they finished building the railroads. People from Italy and Eastern Europe did difficult, low-paying work in factories and smelters. The Irish were often servants to Denver's rich.

Denver's African Americans often held low paying jobs, but many were well-educated businessmen. Their population doubled during World War II when more factories hired them. After the war many joined the fight to get equal rights.

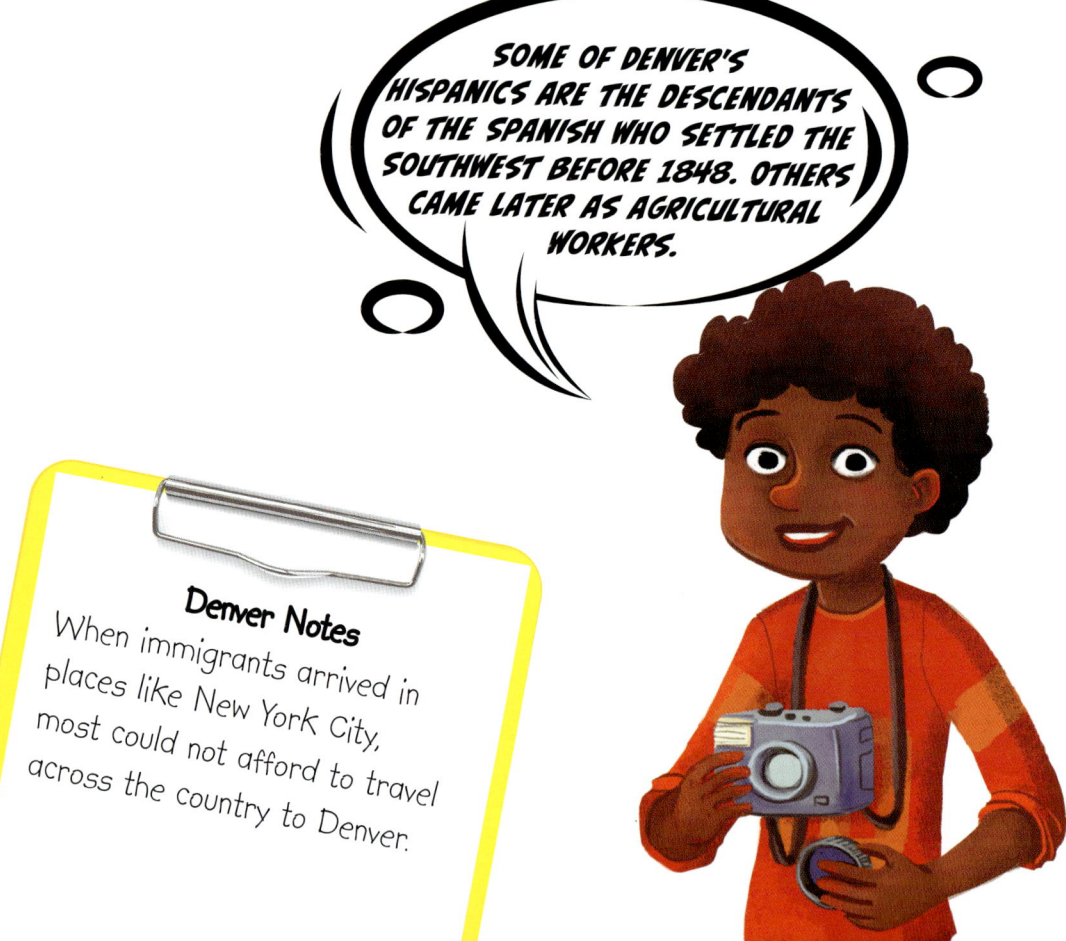

SOME OF DENVER'S HISPANICS ARE THE DESCENDANTS OF THE SPANISH WHO SETTLED THE SOUTHWEST BEFORE 1848. OTHERS CAME LATER AS AGRICULTURAL WORKERS.

Denver Notes
When immigrants arrived in places like New York City, most could not afford to travel across the country to Denver.

The Black American West Museum is in the home of Justina Ford, who was the first black woman doctor in Colorado. Its collection tells the story of black cowboys, the Buffalo Soldiers, and important black businessmen.

African Americans were an important part of America's western history.

Transportation changed Denver. At first, streetcars ran into the country where nobody lived. Roads were improved. Once there were streetcars and roads, towns, houses and stores were built along the routes. These small towns became the **suburbs** of Denver. Denver is now made up of the city and many smaller towns and cities in the five counties around it.

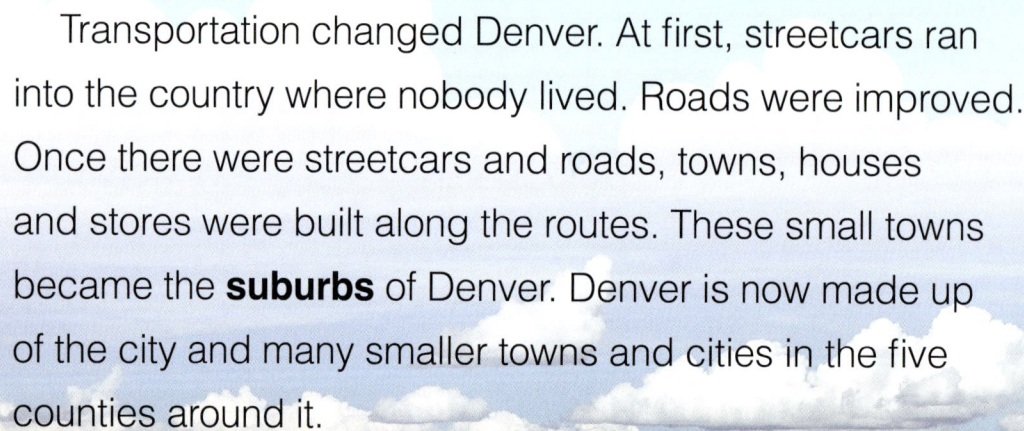

Denver Notes
You can see Mount Evans from Denver. In 1931, the highest paved road in the world was built to its top.

More highways, campgrounds, and parks were built for the many tourists who came to see the beautiful Rocky Mountains. Denver has a large new airport, Denver International Airport.

Denver International Airport is the fifth busiest airport in the United States and the 15th busiest airport in the world.

In 1863, Denver's United States Mint opened to buy gold from miners. Now you can watch them make the coins we use every day.

The United States government built many offices in Denver and nearby suburbs. The Army built bases where soldiers lived and trained. Factories made weapons for war. Many people moved to Denver to work for the government or to make goods for it.

Over the years, smog from smelting blocked the sun. Poisons from some factories seeped into the ground. That changed as factories closed, or cleaned up what was wrong.

Weapons for the U.S. Army were made at Rocky Mountain Arsenal. It is now a nature preserve with bison, prairie dogs, and bald eagles.

These days, people come to Denver for all kinds of reasons. Many are tourists who visit the Rocky Mountains and the city. Others come for meetings, to go shopping, or to watch a football game. This makes downtown a busy place.

Denver has art everywhere, including this 40 foot (12 meter) blue bear looking into the busy downtown convention center.

More to Do

Sports are important in Denver. Many professional sports teams call the Denver region home.

Denver's Professional Sports Teams
- The Colorado Rockies: baseball
- The Denver Broncos: football
- The Colorado Avalanche: hockey
- The Colorado Rapids: soccer
- The Colorado Mammoth: lacrosse
- The Denver Outlaws: lacrosse
- The Denver Nuggets: basketball
- The Denver Barbarians: rugby

Since 1975, Bucky, or Bucko, a 27 foot (8.2 meter) horse, has sat atop first the old and then the new Sports Authority Field at Mile High.

Some people live in Denver because they know they can just look up and see the Rocky Mountains. They know the weather, the crisp air, and the beautiful mountains mean that there are many things to do outside.

Most of the year, the mountains beckon people to come for a drive, a walk, or a long hike. Denver has 14,000 acres (5,666 hectares) of mountain parks outside the city. But you don't have to go to the mountains. Inside Denver are thousands of acres of parks. You can walk, bike, or skate on their miles of trails.

In winter, people head to the mountains to ski, snowboard, and sled. They can ice skate in a city park.

At the Denver Art Museum, you can learn about American Indian art. See paintings of the American West. Play games, do art projects, or borrow a museum backpack full of games, activities, and puzzles.

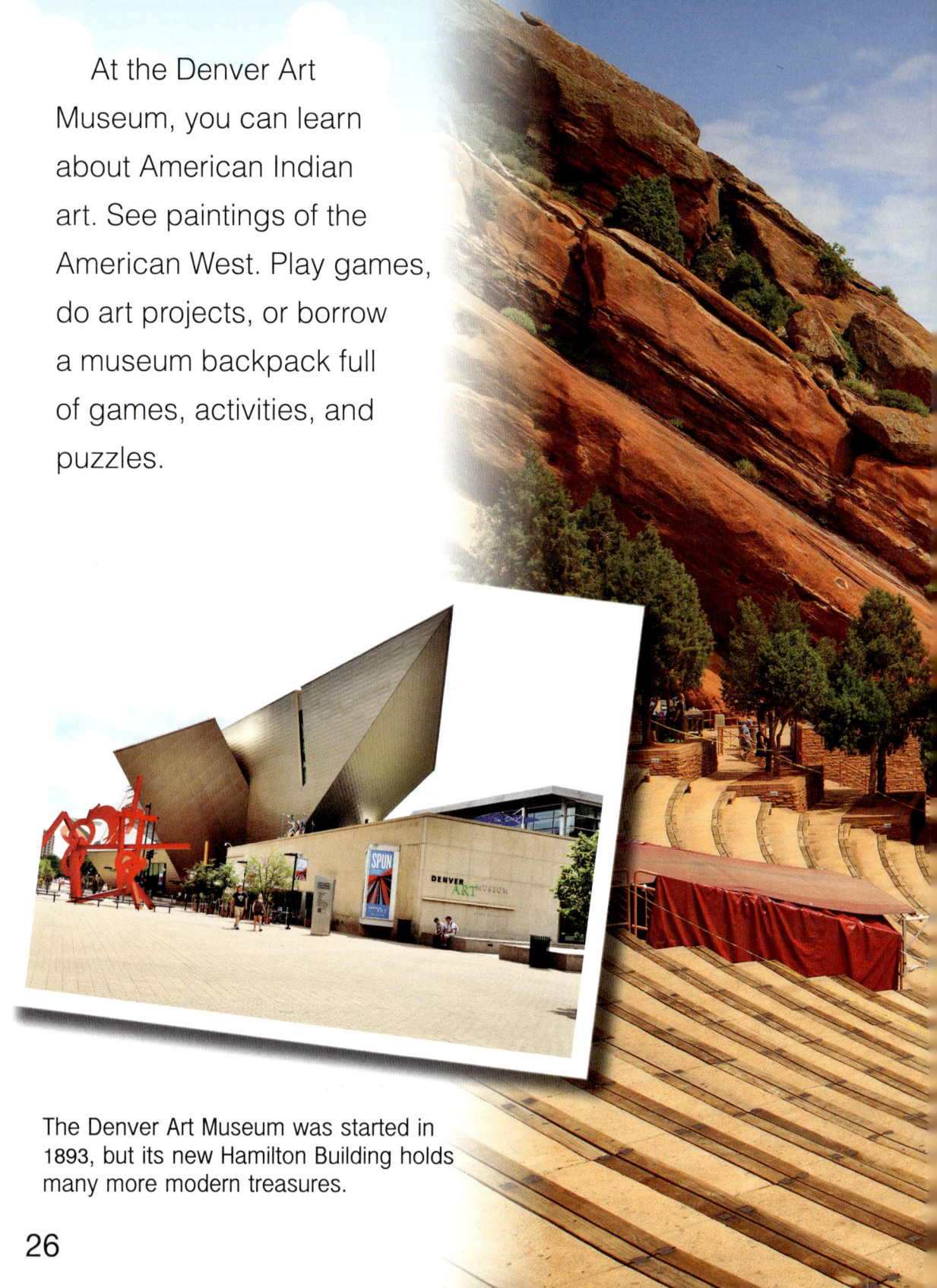

The Denver Art Museum was started in 1893, but its new Hamilton Building holds many more modern treasures.

The Denver Performing Arts Complex is huge. These downtown buildings cover four blocks. It has many theaters. You can watch a play or listen to live musical performances.

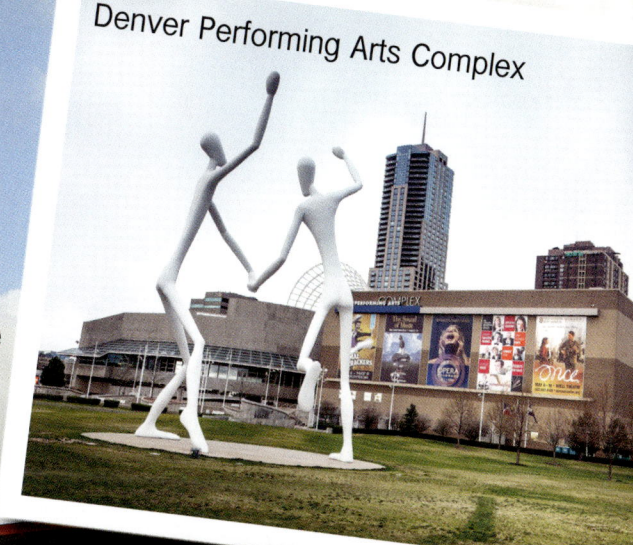
Denver Performing Arts Complex

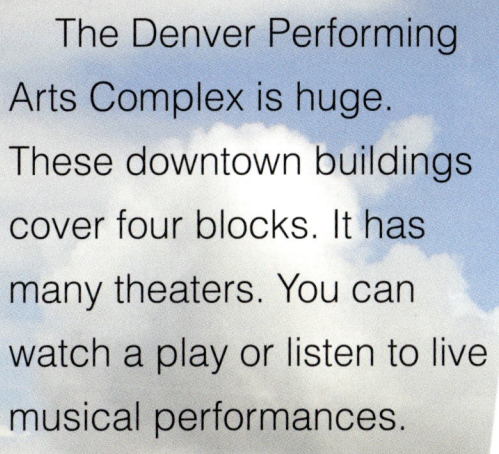

Red Rocks is another concert theater. Although it is outdoors, musicians love the way sounds travel around the rocks.

Parades and festivals in Denver happen all year. In December, it has the world's largest display of holiday lights. There are 40,000 colored lights on government buildings, a trail of lights at the botanic gardens, and a Parade of Lights.

Denver Notes
Elitch Gardens opened in 1890. In 1995 it moved to a new downtown home. It still has exciting roller coasters, water rides, a Ferris wheel, and a hand-carved carousel.

Timeline

1803
The Louisiana Purchase gives most of Colorado to the United States.

1806
Captain Zebulon Pike leads the first U.S. exploring trip into Colorado's Rocky Mountains.

1858
Gold is discovered on the South Platte River.

1859
General William Larimer founds Denver. Gold is found in the nearby Rocky Mountains.

1861
Congress creates the Colorado Territory.

1864
Arapahoe and Cheyenne die in the Sand Creek Massacre.

1870
Railroads connect Denver to the transcontinental railroad and to Kansas.

1876
Colorado becomes the 38th state.

1878
Lots of silver is found in the Rocky Mountains.

1890
A new rush for gold and silver begins.

1893
Women in Colorado win the right to vote.

1906
The U.S. Mint moves to a new building in Denver.

1915
Rocky Mountain National Park established.

1941-45
The Denver region grows into a military center.

1995
Denver International Airport opens.

1998
The Broncos win the Super Bowl.

2001
The Avalanche win the Stanley Cup.

2006
The Denver region's new transportation system (T-Rex) is finished.

2008
Democratic National Convention in Denver nominates an African American, Barack Obama, for president of the United States.

29

Glossary

conflict (KAHN-flikt): a serious disagreement, war, or some other period of fighting

factories (FAK-tur-ees): places where large amounts of something are made by workers and machines

foothills (FUT-hils): low hills at the edge of a mountain range

miners (mine-urs): people who dig minerals out of the ground

ore (or): rock that contains a metal, like gold or silver, or another mineral

plains (playns): large, flat areas of land

smelters (smelt-urs): places where ore is melted so that the metal can be removed

suburbs (SUHB-urbs): areas on the edge of a city with many homes

tourists (TOOR-ists): people who are traveling and visiting a place for pleasure

transcontinental (TRANS-kahn-tuh-NEN-tuhl): across a continent

Index

American Indian(s) 7, 8, 10, 26
bison 5, 21
Colorado 4, 8, 14, 17, 23
dinosaurs 5
farm(s) 9, 11
government 20, 28
miners 11, 12, 20
plains 4, 6, 7, 8, 11, 12
Rocky Mountains 4, 6, 8, 19, 22, 24
sports 23
suburbs 18, 20
tourists 14, 19, 22
travel 6, 14, 16, 18, 19

Show What You Know

1. Describe the land around Denver before it was a city.
2. Why did miners and farmers come into Denver?
3. How did transportation help change Denver?
4. How has the Rocky Mountain Arsenal changed?
5. What are five things to do outdoors in and around Denver?

Websites to Visit

www.historycolorado.org/kids-students/kids-students
www.usmint.gov/kids
www.denvergov.org/content/denvergov/en/denver-parks-and-recreation/parks.html

About the Author

Hilarie Staton loves to travel and recently visited Denver and the nearby Rocky Mountains. When she's home, she writes about people, places, and history. She has written many books for kids.

Meet The Author!
www.meetREMauthors.com

© 2017 Rourke Educational Media

All rights reserved. No part of this book may be reproduced or utilized in any form or by any means, electronic or mechanical including photocopying, recording, or by any information storage and retrieval system without permission in writing from the publisher.

www.rourkeeducationalmedia.com

PHOTO CREDITS: Cover: skyline © photo.ua-Shutterstock.com cityscape-Shutterstock.com, Red Rocks amphitheater © Sharion Lambdin | Dreamstime.com; rodeo © Lincoln Rogers-Shutterstock.com, family in snow © gorillaimages-Shutterstock.com; page 5 inset photo © Footwarrior https://creativecommons.org/licenses/by-sa/3.0/deed.en ; page 7 courtesy of Walters Musem, painting Commissioned by William T. Walters, 1858-1860; map page 8 © © Shannon1, Wikipedia, stagecoach page 8 courtesy of Library of Congress; pages 10-11 Sandcreek © chapin31-istockphoto.com; page 15 Molly Brown Museum © Pkorchagina | Dreamstime.com; page 22 © © Nyker1 | Dreamstime.com; page 26 Art Museum © © Eq Roy | Dreamstime.com, pages 26-27 Red Rocks amphitheater © Sharion Lambdin | Dreamstime.com; page 28 © Arinahabich08 | Dreamstime.com

Other photos from Shutterstock.com: Colorado map_p3 © Rainer Lesniewski; pages 4-5 © EdgeOfReason; pages 6-7 © Shane Wilson Link; page 9 © George Allen Penton; page 11 © Lincoln Rogers; pages 12-13 © Ambient Ideas; page 14-15 Capitol building © Jeff Zehnder; page 17 © Everett Historical; pages 18-19 Evans Road © Hikeflyshoot, page 19 airport © Arina P Habich; page 20 © Henryk Sadura, page 21 bison © Tom Potter, eagle © Dawn Wilson Photo; page 23 © photo.ua; pages 24-25 © Arina P Habich; page 27 inset photo © photo.ua

Edited by: Keli Sipperley
Cover and interior design by: Nicola Stratford, www.nicolastratford.com
Illustrations by: Caroline Romanet

Library of Congress PCN Data

Dropping in on Denver / Hilarie Staton
ISBN 978-1-68342-173-3 (hard cover)
ISBN 978-1-68342-210-5 (soft cover)
ISBN 978-1-68342-240-2 (e-Book)
Library of Congress Control Number: 2016956595

Also Available as:
ROURKE'S e-Books

Printed in the United States of America, North Mankato, Minnesota